· T R O P H I E S ·

Spelling
Practice
Book

Grade 2

Harcourt

Orlando   Boston   Dallas   Chicago   San Diego

Visit *The Learning Site!*
www.harcourtschool.com

Contents

Contents

Making Your Spelling Log

This book gives you a place to keep a word list of your own. It is called a **SPELLING LOG!**

If you need some **IDEAS** for creating your list, just look at what I usually do!

While I read, I look for **INTERESTING WORDS.** I listen for **NEW WORDS** used by people, too.

I include words that I need to use when I **WRITE,** especially words that are hard for me to spell.

Before I put a word in my Spelling Log, I check the spelling. I look up the word in a **DICTIONARY,** or I ask for help.

To help me understand and remember the meaning of my word, I write a **DEFINITION** or draw a picture. I also use the word in a sentence.

Here's how you use it!

THE SPELLING LOG SECTION in this book is just for you. It is your own list of words that you want to remember. Your Spelling Log has three parts. Here's how to use each part.

Spelling Words to Study

This is where you will list words from each lesson that you need to study. Write the words you misspell on the Pretest. Add other words you are not sure you can always spell correctly.

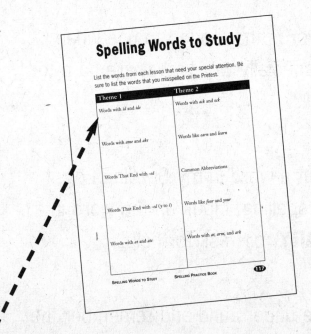

This handy list makes it easy for me to study the words I need to learn!

I write a clue beside each word to help me remember it.

My Own Word Collection

You choose the words to list on these pages. Include new words, interesting words, and any other words you want to remember. You choose how to group them, too!

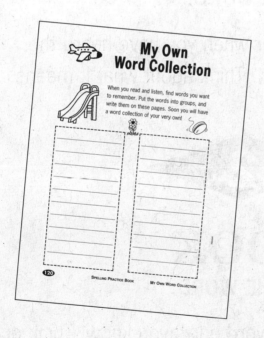

© Harcourt

Study Steps to Learn a Word

Check out these steps.

SAY
THE WORD.

Remember when you have heard the word used. Think about what it means.

LOOK
AT THE WORD.

Find any word parts you know. Think of another word that has a meaning or spelling like it. Picture the word in your mind.

© Harcourt

SPELL
THE WORD TO YOURSELF.

Think about the way each sound is spelled.

WRITE
THE WORD WHILE YOU ARE LOOKING AT IT.

Check the way you have formed your letters. If you have not written the word clearly or correctly, write it again.

CHECK
WHAT YOU HAVE LEARNED.

Cover the word and write it. If you have not spelled the word correctly, practice these steps until you can write it correctly every time.

© Harcourt

Words with *id* and *ide*

▶ Write a Spelling Word from the box to complete each sentence.

hide	slide	wide
pride	bid	eyelid	inside

1. Ian takes _____ in his work.

2. Barb went _____ to stay warm.

3. Our dog Max likes to _____ bones.

4. Julio likes to _____ to second base.

5. Will you place a _____ at the fair?

6. That truck makes _____ turns.

7. Why is my _____ red and sore?

▶ On each line, write a Spelling Word from the box.

hid	ride	kid

8. _____   9. _____

10. _____

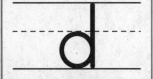
© Harcourt

Name_____

► Which Spelling Words do not look right?
Circle the misspelled word in each row.
Then write it correctly on the line.

1. ride   eet   bid   _____

2. bigg   hide   wide   _____

3. slide   hid   peeple   _____

4. noh   pride   ride   _____

► Write these Spelling Words in ABC
order.

| ride | pride | hide | wide | bid | brown |

5. _____   **6.** _____

7. _____   **8.** _____

9. _____   **10.** _____

1. hide
2. slide
3. ride
4. wide
5. pride
6. bid
7. kid
8. eyelid
9. inside
10. hid
11. no
12. big
13. brown
14. eat
15. people

SPELLING STRATEGY

Checking Spelling

After you write something, read what you wrote. Use a dictionary to check the spelling of words you are not sure of.

SPELLING WORDS

1. hide
2. slide
3. ride
4. wide
5. pride
6. bid
7. kid
8. eyelid
9. inside
10. hid
11. no
12. big
13. brown
14. eat
15. people

▶ **Word Scramble** Unscramble the letters to write the Spelling Words.

1. sidein   _____

2. loeepp   _____

3. bwnro   _____

4. eidley   _____

▶ **Write the Words** Write the missing letters in each Spelling Word. Then write the Spelling Word.

5. i ____ ____ ____ ____ e   _____

6. ____ y ____ ____ i ____   _____

7. p ____ opl ____   _____

▶ **Change a Letter** Change one letter in each word to make a Spelling Word. Circle the letter you are changing. Then write the Spelling Word.

8. bit   _____

9. wife   _____

10. glide   _____

11. ripe   _____

SPELLING PRACTICE BOOK

LESSON 1

© Harcourt

Name _____

Words with *ame* and *ake*

▶ Use a Spelling Word from the box to label each picture.

same	games	flame
snake	take	brake	name

1. _____

2. _____

3. _____

4. _____

5. _____

6. _____

7. _____

▶ On each line, write the Spelling Word again.

8. make _____

9. became _____

10. mistake _____

SPELLING WORDS

1. games
2. take
3. make
4. name
5. flame
6. same
7. became
8. brake
9. snake
10. mistake
11. eyelid
12. slide
13. line
14. more
15. together

Handwriting Tip: When you write the letter *a*, make a circle that touches the midline, like this:

_____

a

1. games
2. take
3. make
4. name
5. flame
6. same
7. became
8. brake
9. snake
10. mistake
11. eyelid
12. slide
13. line
14. more
15. together

SPELLING STRATEGY

Sounds and Letters

Often a sound can be written two or more ways.

Name _____

▶ **Circle the correct spelling. Then write the Spelling Word on the line.**

1. ilid   eilid   eyelid   _____

2. twogether   together   toogether

_____

3. more   mohr   mor   _____

4. slide   slied   slyed   _____

▶ **Circle the correct Spelling Word to complete each sentence. Then write the correct Spelling Word on the line.**

5. We can (tayke, take) our bicycles with

us. _____

6. Let's (make, maike) a pie. _____

7. Put out the (flame, flayme) before

leaving the camp. _____

8. We can play (games, gaimes) like

checkers and hide-and-seek. _____

9. In the fall, the leaves (becayme,

became) red and yellow. _____

© Harcourt

Name _____

▶ **Ask Me a Question** Answer each question with a Spelling Word.

1. Which word means "something wrong"? _____

2. Which word has the word *be* in it? _____

3. Which word means "not alone"? _____

4. Which word is an animal? _____

5. Which word describes something on your face? _____

▶ **Word Search** Circle six Spelling Words in the puzzle. The words can go across or down. Then write the words on the lines.

6. _____ 7. _____

8. _____ 9. _____

10. _____ 11. _____

SPELLING WORDS

1. games
2. take
3. make
4. name
5. flame
6. same
7. became
8. brake
9. snake
10. mistake
11. eyelid
12. slide
13. line
14. more
15. together

```
f l a m e t t
a n t i g n o
r b o s r l g
e m i t o m e
b e c a m e t
s n a k e l h
w u n e s p e
e y e l i d r
```

© Harcourt

1. barked
2. licked
3. backed
4. thanked
5. painted
6. opened
7. mailed
8. remarked
9. checked
10. finished
11. mistake
12. became
13. about
14. few
15. same

Handwriting Tip: When you write a word, make sure all of the letters sit on the bottom line. Also, make sure the letters are not too close together or too far apart.

Name _____

Words That End with -ed

▶ Complete the story. Write a Spelling Word from the box on each line.

| finished thanked opened mailed |
| checked licked painted |

When Josie **(1)** _____ writing to her

grandpa, she **(2)** _____ her letter for

mistakes. She signed it and **(3)** _____

the envelope to close it. Josie also

(4) _____ a design on the envelope.

Then she walked with her mom to the

corner and **(5)** _____ the letter. When

her grandpa **(6)** _____ it, he was so

happy. He called and **(7)** _____ Josie.

▶ Write each Spelling Word from the box on a line.

| remarked backed barked |

8. _____   9. _____

10. _____

© Harcourt

SPELLING PRACTICE BOOK

LESSON 3

Name_____

► **Find the Spelling Word that fits the clue and shape. Write the word in the shape.**

1. alike

2. turned into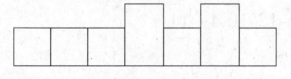

3. something wrong

4. not many

5. around

► **Proofread each sentence. Circle the Spelling Words that are misspelled. Write the words correctly on the lines.**

6. I cheked the card and saw it was from Uncle Bill. _____

7. Mom remarcked that the box had holes in it. _____

8. Inside, something barkt! _____

1. barked
2. licked
3. backed
4. thanked
5. painted
6. opened
7. mailed
8. remarked
9. checked
10. finished
11. mistake
12. became
13. about
14. few
15. same

SPELLING
STRATEGY
Picture a Word and Sound It Out
When sounding out words with endings like *-ed*, picture the way the word looks without its ending. Then add the ending.

© Harcourt

SPELLING WORDS

1. barked
2. licked
3. backed
4. thanked
5. painted
6. opened
7. mailed
8. remarked
9. checked
10. finished
11. mistake
12. became
13. about
14. few
15. same

Name _____

▶ **Crack the Code** Use the code to spell Spelling Words.

1 = e	2 = s	3 = i	4 = n	5 = d
6 = a	7 = k	8 = p	9 = m	10 = o
11 = t	12 = b	13 = t	14 = u	15 = c

1. 9-3-2-13-6-7-1 _____

2. 6-12-10-14-11 _____

3. 12-1-15-6-9-1 _____

4. 10-8-1-4-1-5 _____

▶ **Try This Crossword Puzzle!** Read the clues, and write the Spelling Words in the puzzle.

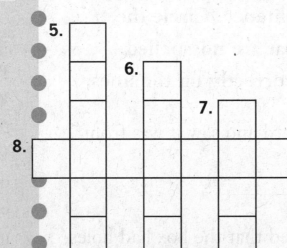

DOWN

5. made a comment
6. ended
7. turned into

ACROSS

8. made a picture with paints
9. the opposite of closed

Name _____

Words That End with -ed (*y* to *i*)

▶ Complete the story. Write a Spelling Word from the box on each line.

tried	studied	worried	hurried
cried	copied	replied	

Lisa was (**1**) _____ about her big

concert. She (**2**) _____ the music each

night for hours. She (**3**) _____ the

music on paper so she could look at it all the

time. On the day of the show, Lisa

(**4**) _____ to the concert hall. She

(**5**) _____ hard to play well. When it

was over, the audience (**6**) _____ with

cheers and applause.

▶ Write each Spelling Word from the box on a line.

fried	carried

7. _____   8. _____

LESSON 4   **SPELLING PRACTICE BOOK**

19

© Harcourt

1. cried
2. hurried
3. replied
4. fried
5. tried
6. worried
7. carried
8. copied
9. married
10. studied
11. remarked
12. finished
13. alone
14. river
15. think

Handwriting Tip: Remember when writing an *i* to put the dot above the line.

_____

- - - - - - ● - - - - - -
|

SPELLING WORDS

1. cried
2. hurried
3. replied
4. fried
5. tried
6. worried
7. carried
8. copied
9. married
10. studied
11. remarked
12. finished
13. alone
14. river
15. think

SPELLING STRATEGY

Use a Dictionary

If you need help, use a dictionary. Dictionary entries show the spelling of word endings.

▶ **Add the ending *-ed* to each word. Write the Spelling Word.**

1. reply _____   **2.** try _____

3. study _____   **4.** copy _____

5. cry _____

▶ **Circle the word that is correct. Then write the Spelling Word on a line. You may want to check a dictionary if you are not sure which answer is correct.**

6. Mom (**finnished, finished**) cooking the

fish for dinner. _____

7. Katie and I raced home from the (**river,**

rivur). _____

8. My grandparents (**think, thinck**)

reading is important. _____

9. Clint (**remarked, remarkd**) that he

had a dog. _____

10. Dad went for a walk (**aloan, alone**).

_____

© Harcourt

Name_____

▶ **Picture Words** Write a Spelling Word that tells what happened in each picture.

1. _____

2. _____

3. _____

4. _____

▶ **Word Scramble** Unscramble the letters to write the Spelling Words.

5. nealo _____

6. hedinifs _____

7. verri _____

▶ **Try These Word Clues!** Write a Spelling Word for each clue.

8. I am concerned. I am _____.

9. They are husband and wife. They are

_____.

10. He answered. He _____.

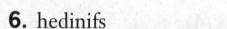

© Harcourt

SPELLING WORDS

1. cried
2. hurried
3. replied
4. fried
5. tried
6. worried
7. carried
8. copied
9. married
10. studied
11. remarked
12. finished
13. alone
14. river
15. think

SPELLING WORDS

1. sat
2. ate
3. acrobat
4. flat
5. that
6. fat
7. gate
8. appreciate
9. create
10. state
11. worried
12. studied
13. children
14. each
15. girl

Handwriting Tip: When you write, hold your pencil about an inch above the point. Hold it between your thumb and pointer finger.

Words with *at* and *ate*

▶ Finish the letter. Write a Spelling Word from the box on each line.

sat	acrobat	appreciate	ate
flat	fat	gate	that

Dear Rudy,

   Thanks for inviting me to the circus. I really **(1)** _____ it! My excitement began the moment I passed through the

(2) _____. The spot where we

(3) _____ had a great view. I was

amazed when the **(4)** _____ clown walked the tightrope. I was sure

(5) _____ he would fall **(6)** _____ on his face! I think he was really an

(7) _____. Even though I

(8) _____ too much popcorn, I had a great time. Thanks again.

       Your pal,

       Kristy

Name _____

► **Add the missing letters to complete each Spelling Word. Then write the Spelling Words.**

1. ch __ l __ __ e n   _____

2. g __ r __   _____

3. __ __ c h   _____

4. s __ u __ i __ d   _____

5. w __ __ __ i __ d   _____

► **Picture a word's shape to help you spell it. Write a Spelling Word in each word shape.**

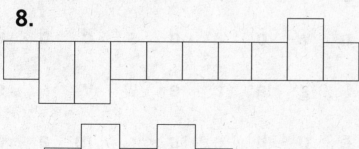

6.

7.

8.

9.

SPELLING WORDS

1. sat
2. ate
3. acrobat
4. flat
5. that
6. fat
7. gate
8. appreciate
9. create
10. state
11. worried
12. studied
13. children
14. each
15. girl

SPELLING
STRATEGY
Study Steps to Learn a New Word

To learn to spell any new word, say it, look at it, spell it aloud, write it, then check your spelling.

© Harcourt

SPELLING WORDS

1. sat
2. ate
3. acrobat
4. flat
5. that
6. fat
7. gate
8. appreciate
9. create
10. state
11. worried
12. studied
13. children
14. each
15. girl

▶ **Word Clues** Complete each sentence with a Spelling Word.

1. When I make something, I _____ it.

2. I _____ the gifts I got for my birthday.

3. An _____ can perform amazing tricks.

4. He _____ that he would lose.

5. They _____ for the test.

▶ **Word Search** Circle six Spelling Words in the puzzle.

t	r	n	a	c	r	o	b	a	t
h	s	o	e	r	l	f	p	k	m
a	p	p	r	e	c	i	a	t	e
t	n	w	o	a	d	s	q	d	z
r	l	g	a	t	e	w	v	j	s
d	e	u	h	e	s	r	m	a	p
y	c	h	i	l	d	r	e	n	p

© Harcourt

Practice Test

A. Read each sentence. Find the correctly spelled word that completes the sentence. Fill in the circle in front of that word.

Example: I _____ to run faster than Ben.

⚬ tride   ⚫ tried   ⚬ tryed

1. We _____ our fence this weekend.

⚬ painted   ⚬ painnted   ⚬ panted

2. My aunt and uncle were _____ in May.

⚬ maried   ⚬ married   ⚬ marryed

3. Last night I _____ reading my book.

⚬ finished   ⚬ finnished   ⚬ finishd

4. The _____ can walk on a tightrope.

⚬ acrobate   ⚬ accrobat   ⚬ acrobat

5. The winner _____ all of the voters.

⚬ thanked   ⚬ thankt   ⚬ thancked

6. I _____ a window to let in some air.

⚬ opend   ⚬ openned   ⚬ opened

7. The next day she _____ to my letter.

⚬ replied   ⚬ replyed   ⚬ repleid

© Harcourt

Name _____

B. Read each sentence. Is the spelling of the underlined word correct or incorrect? Fill in the circle in front of your answer.

Example: Many people have <u>pride</u> in their country.

⬤ correct   ◯ incorrect

1. We <u>appreciait</u> all your hard work.
   ◯ correct   ◯ incorrect

2. I put on two different socks by <u>mistake</u>.
   ◯ correct   ◯ incorrect

3. I like to <u>create</u> shapes and figures with clay.
   ◯ correct   ◯ incorrect

4. When summer arrived, the weather <u>became</u> hot.
   ◯ correct   ◯ incorrect

5. Many people <u>remarcked</u> on my new outfit.
   ◯ correct   ◯ incorrect

6. I <u>checked</u> the oven before we left the house.
   ◯ correct   ◯ incorrect

7. Mom <u>worried</u> about us coming home late.
   ◯ correct   ◯ incorrect

© Harcourt

Name_____

Words with *ack* and *ock*

▶ Look at each picture. Then write the Spelling Word that names the picture.

1. _____ 2.  _____

3. _____ 4. _____

5. _____ 6. _____

7. _____

▶ Write each Spelling Word from the box on a line.

shock	flock	rocket

8. _____ 9. _____

10. _____

1. black
2. pack
3. crack
4. snack
5. horseback
6. lock
7. rocket
8. flock
9. shock
10. clock
11. appreciate
12. acrobat
13. grow
14. last
15. mouse

Handwriting Tip: When you write an *o*, be sure to start a little below the midline and close the letter completely so that your *o* does not look like a *c*.

1. black
2. pack
3. crack
4. snack
5. horseback
6. lock
7. rocket
8. flock
9. shock
10. clock
11. appreciate
12. acrobat
13. grow
14. last
15. mouse

SPELLING STRATEGY

Checking Spelling

After you have written something, read what you wrote. If you are not sure how to spell a word, check it.

Name _____

▶ **Circle the correct spelling of each Spelling Word. Then write the word correctly on the line.**

1. clok   clock   _____

2. flock   floock   _____

3. mousse   mouse   _____

4. grow   groe   _____

▶ **Proofread Anita's letter. Circle the six spelling errors. Then write the words correctly on the lines.**

Dear Grandma,

   Here is a picture of me on horsebake. This blac mare looks nice, but when she heard the crak of a twig, she took off like a rockett! It was quite a shook. After I gave her a snak, she calmed down. As you can tell, our trip to the ranch has been exciting!

                    Love,
                    Anita

5. _____   6. _____

7. _____   8. _____

9. _____   10. _____

© Harcourt

Name _____

▶ **What Am I?** Write the Spelling Word that answers each riddle.

1. I swing in a circus.

   I'm an ac ____ ____ ____ at.

   _____

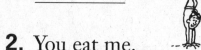

2. You eat me.

   I'm a s ____ ____ ____ k. _____

3. I like cheese.

   I'm a mo ____ ____ ____ . _____

4. I'm riding a horse.

   I'm on horseb ____ ____ ____ .

   _____

▶ **Change a Letter** Change one letter in each word to make a Spelling Word. Circle the letter. Then write the Spelling Word.

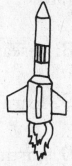

5. stock   _____

6. look   _____

7. racket   _____

SPELLING WORDS

1. black
2. pack
3. crack
4. snack
5. horseback
6. lock
7. rocket
8. flock
9. shock
10. clock
11. appreciate
12. acrobat
13. grow
14. last
15. mouse

© Harcourt

1. learn
2. earnest
3. earth
4. heard
5. pearl
6. search
7. rehearse
8. earn
9. yearn
10. research
11. horseback
12. rocket
13. early
14. pretty
15. someone

Handwriting Tip: When you write the letter *r*, be sure to stop at the midline so that your *r* does not look like an *n*.

r n

Name _____

Words like *earn* and *learn*

▶ **Complete each sentence with a Spelling Word from the box.**

pearl	earn	earnest	search
yearn	heard	rehearse	

1. Let's _____ for more clues.

2. I _____ a new song yesterday.

3. We can _____ for the play after school.

4. I want to _____ some extra money.

5. I _____ for warm weather in winter.

6. Mom wears a _____ necklace.

7. His apology was _____ .

▶ **On each line, write the Spelling Word again.**

8. research _____

9. learn _____

10. earth _____

© Harcourt

Name _____

▶ **Circle the Spelling Words that look right. Check them with the list. Then write the correct word on the line.**

1. heard   herde   _____

2. yarne   yearn   _____

▶ **Use Spelling Words to complete the story. Write the correct spelling.**

One **(3)** (erly, early) _____ morning,

I found a **(4)** (pearl, purl) _____ in my backyard! It had been buried in the

(5) (earth, erth) _____. When I showed it to Mom, she said, "Now I can

stop my **(6)** (serch, search) _____. I've been looking for that all week!"

▶ **Dictionary** Write these Spelling Words in ABC order.

| learn | pretty | horseback | rocket |

7. _____   **8.** _____

9. _____   **10.** _____

SPELLING WORDS

1. learn
2. earnest
3. earth
4. heard
5. pearl
6. search
7. rehearse
8. earn
9. yearn
10. research
11. horseback
12. rocket
13. early
14. pretty
15. someone

SPELLING
STRATEGY
Comparing Spellings

When you are not sure how to spell a word, try writing it in different ways. Choose the way that looks correct.

© Harcourt

1. learn
2. earnest
3. earth
4. heard
5. pearl
6. search
7. rehearse
8. earn
9. yearn
10. research
11. horseback
12. rocket
13. early
14. pretty
15. someone

Name _____

▶ **Word Math** Add or subtract the letters shown. Write the Spelling Word.

   1. some + one = _____

   2. reheat - t + rse = _____

   3. reseat - t + rch = _____

▶ **A Puzzle** Read the clues, and write the Spelling Words in the puzzle.

DOWN

4. look up information

6. the ground

ACROSS

5. practice for a play or concert

7. arriving before expected

▶ **Write the Words** Add letters to make Spelling Words.

r e ____ e a ____ ____ h

____ e h e ____ r s ____

   8. _____   **9.** _____

© Harcourt

Name _____

Common Abbreviations

▶ Complete the letter using the Spelling Words.

| Mr. | Mrs. | Dr. | Jan. | St. | Dec. |

Mary Fisher
Spring Street Elementary School

111 Spring **(1)** _____
Springville, MA 02999

(2) _____ 31, 2002

Dear **(3)** _____ Fisher,

   Please excuse my son Corey from

school **(4)** _____ 2. He will be seeing

his doctor, **(5)** _____ Michael Lee.

   Sincerely,

(6) _____ Steven Perry

SPELLING WORDS

1. Mr.
2. Mrs.
3. Dr.
4. Jan.
5. Aug.
6. Dec.
7. Tues.
8. Wed.
9. Sun.
10. St.
11. rehearse
12. search
13. before
14. blue
15. room

Handwriting Tip: When you write a period, be sure it sits on the bottom line and is not too small or too large.

© Harcourt

1. Mr.
2. Mrs.
3. Dr.
4. Jan.
5. Aug.
6. Dec.
7. Tues.
8. Wed.
9. Sun.
10. St.
11. rehearse
12. search
13. before
14. blue
15. room

SPELLING STRATEGY

Strategies for Abbreviating

Remember that abbreviations of proper nouns and titles must begin with a capital letter.

Name _____

► **Match the Spelling Word to the word it abbreviates. Then write the abbreviation.**

Wed.	August	1. _____
Dr.	Sunday	2. _____
Mr.	Doctor	3. _____
Sun.	Wednesday	4. _____
Aug.	Mister	5. _____

► **Which is the correct way to abbreviate? Circle the correct abbreviation. Then write it on the line.**

6.	Srt.	St.	st.	_____
7.	Dec.	Dece.	dec.	_____
8.	Tus.	Tues	Tues.	_____
9.	Jan.	Jry.	janu.	_____
10.	Mss.	Mrs.	Mrs	_____

© Harcourt

Name_____

▶ **ABC Order** Write these Spelling Words in ABC order. Circle the ones that are titles for people.

| room   Mrs.   before   search   Dr. |

1. _____   2. _____

3. _____   4. _____

5. _____

▶ **Clues** Write the Spelling Word described in each clue.

6. the color of the sky   _____

7. the title for a man   _____

8. a weekend day   _____

9. to get ready for a play   _____

10. the first month of the year _____

© Harcourt

SPELLING WORDS

1. Mr.
2. Mrs.
3. Dr.
4. Jan.
5. Aug.
6. Dec.
7. Tues.
8. Wed.
9. Sun.
10. St.
11. rehearse
12. search
13. before
14. blue
15. room

1. four
2. poured
3. your
4. course
5. court
6. fourteen
7. mourn
8. source
9. fourth
10. resource
11. Dr.
12. St.
13. smell
14. thank
15. open

Handwriting Tip: When you write an *o*, be sure to close the circle completely so that it does not look like a *u*.

Name _____

Words like *four* and *your*

▶ **Match the Spelling Words to the clues. Write the Spelling Word on each line.**

four	your	fourth	court
poured	source	fourteen	

1. a place where you play basketball

   _____

2. the number after thirteen _____

3. put liquid in a cup _____

4. belonging to you _____

5. place something comes from _____

6. the place after third _____

7. the number before five _____

▶ **On each line, write the Spelling Word again.**

8. course _____

9. mourn _____

10. resource _____

© Harcourt

Name_____

▶ **Write a Spelling Word that rhymes with the underlined word and makes sense in the sentence.**

1. The _____ of us rode from <u>shore</u> by canoe.

2. We traveled <u>north</u> on the _____ day.

3. Although the rain _____ down, our hearts <u>soared</u>.

4. Using our own <u>force</u>, we stayed on _____.

5. With our map as a <u>resource</u> we found the river's _____.

▶ **Circle the word in each group that is misspelled. Then write the Spelling Word correctly on the line.**

6. open   moorn   fourth   _____

7. four   St.   recource   _____

8. poured   forteen   course   _____

SPELLING WORDS

1. four
2. poured
3. your
4. course
5. court
6. fourteen
7. mourn
8. source
9. fourth
10. resource
11. Dr.
12. St.
13. smell
14. thank
15. open

SPELLING STRATEGY

Rhyming Words

Think about the sound of the word. Does it rhyme with another word you know?

© Harcourt

SPELLING WORDS

1. four
2. poured
3. your
4. course
5. court
6. fourteen
7. mourn
8. source
9. fourth
10. resource
11. Dr.
12. St.
13. smell
14. thank
15. open

Name _____

▶ **Unscramble these Spelling Words.**

1. truefeno _____

2. userreco _____

3. srouec _____

4. odeupr _____

▶ **Fun With Words** Find five Spelling Words in the puzzle. Circle each one. Then write the words on the lines.

```
c a n i d f m e
o h e z y o d r
u g m c a u k l
r e s o u r c e
t u j u w t y s
s o u r c e p g
a d n s i e h v
w p u e f n l y
```

5. _____   6. _____

7. _____   8. _____

9. _____

© Harcourt

Name _____

Words with *ar*, *arm*, and *ark*

▶ **Finish the letter. Write a Spelling Word from the box on each line.**

| star farm jar charm bar dark sparkle |

Dear Mom and Dad,

    Aunt Judy's place is full of

(1) _____ . Last night we arrived at the

(2) _____ when it was **(3)** _____ . I

almost didn't see the wooden **(4)** _____
on the barn door! Still, we could see every

(5) _____ in the sky. You should have

seen them **(6)** _____ ! I wish I could put

them in a **(7)** _____ and take them
home with me. I love it here!

                 Love,
                 Heidi

© Harcourt

SPELLING WORDS

1. bar
2. jar
3. star
4. farm
5. harm
6. charm
7. dark
8. remark
9. sparkle
10. alarm
11. fourteen
12. source
13. between
14. enough
15. idea

Handwriting Tip: When writing *r* and *m* next to each other, be sure that they do not touch.

1. bar
2. jar
3. star
4. farm
5. harm
6. charm
7. dark
8. remark
9. sparkle
10. alarm
11. fourteen
12. source
13. between
14. enough
15. idea

SPELLING
STRATEGY

Using a Dictionary

After you write something, check your spelling. Circle words you are not sure of. Then check the spelling of those words in the dictionary.

Name _____

▶ **Write a spelling word for each clue.**

    1. I wake you up in the morning.

      I'm an _____.

    2. I come with peanut butter inside me.

      I'm a _____.

    3. I'm a cow.

      I live on a _____.

    4. I'm the moon.

      I come out when it's _____.

▶ **Complete the story with the correct Spelling Words. Write each word on the line.**

Grandpa and I had an **(5)** (ide, idea)

_____. We thought it would be fun to

catch fireflies in a **(6)** (jar, jarr) _____.
We waited until it got **(7)** (dark, darc)

_____. **(8)** (Beetwen, Between)

_____ the two of us, we caught

(9) (fourteen, fourten) _____.

                                          LESSON 5

© Harcourt

Name _____

▶ **Word Shapes** Find the Spelling Word that fits the clue and shape. Write the word in the shape.

1. comment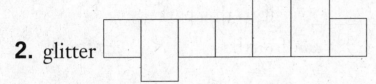

2. glitter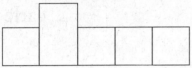

3. something that wakes you up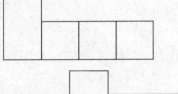

4. a place where animals live

5. danger

▶ **Word Math** Add or subtract the letters shown. Write the Spelling Word.

6. fo + urtu - tu + teen = _____

7. spackle - c + r = _____

8. bee - e + tween = _____

9. enou + gh = _____

10. dart - t + k = _____

SPELLING WORDS

1. bar
2. jar
3. star
4. farm
5. harm
6. charm
7. dark
8. remark
9. sparkle
10. alarm
11. fourteen
12. source
13. between
14. enough
15. idea

© Harcourt

Name _____

Practice Test

A. Read each sentence. Find the correctly spelled word that completes the sentence. Fill in the circle in front of that word.

Example: This is my _____ visit to this park.

   ⬭ forth   ⬛ fourth   ⬭ fouth

1. We need to arrive _____.

   ⬭ early   ⬭ erly   ⬭ earle

2. I can help you do the _____.

   ⬭ research   ⬭ reserch   ⬭ researck

3. What _____ did she make?

   ⬭ remarck   ⬭ remak   ⬭ remark

4. Rain _____ down all day.

   ⬭ pored   ⬭ pourd   ⬭ poured

5. The note was dated "_____, Nov. 3."

   ⬭ Tues.   ⬭ Tus.   ⬭ Tuse.

6. They went to space in a _____.

   ⬭ roket   ⬭ rocket   ⬭ rockit

7. There are _____ students in the class.

   ⬭ forteen   ⬭ fourteen   ⬭ fourtine

© Harcourt

Name _____

B. Read each sentence. Find the underlined Spelling Word that is spelled correctly. Fill in the circle below it.

Example: In the darc I tripped on my alarm.
               ◯   ━

1. I rode on horsback on the farm.
              ◯   ◯

2. I herd his remark.
   ◯   ◯

3. We start to rehearse in Janu.
         ◯   ◯

4. There is one black sheep in the flok.
        ◯   ◯

5. The fourth day of Aug we go on vacation.
      ◯   ◯

6. That sparckle you see is a star.
     ◯   ◯

7. Mrs. Lincoln is a good recource for news.
   ◯   ◯

8. He is impressed by yor charm.
        ◯ ◯

9. I can earn extra credit in this cource.
   ◯   ◯

10. I got a shock when I looked at the clook.
     ◯   ◯

© Harcourt

1. pioneers
2. cheers
3. clearing
4. hear
5. nearby
6. year
7. beard
8. reindeer
9. steer
10. peer
11. remark
12. alarm
13. sleep
14. country
15. rain

Handwriting Tip: When writing short letters, such as *e*, *a*, and *r*, remember that they should touch the midline.

_____

Name _____

Words with *ear* and *eer*

▶ Complete the sentences. Write a Spelling Word from the box on each line.

nearby	year	reindeer	hear
steer	clearing	pioneers	

1. One day last _____, we saw an amazing sight.

2. We were driving past a _____.

3. Suddenly, we saw some _____!

4. Dad almost forgot to _____ the car.

5. I _____ they are not there anymore.

6. I wonder if they are still _____.

7. _____ rode in covered wagons.

▶ On each line, write the Spelling Word again.

8. peer _____ 9. beard _____

10. cheers _____

© Harcourt

Name _____

▶ Circle the Spelling Words that look right. Check each word with the list. Then rewrite the correct word on the line.

1. cheers   chears   _____

2. beerd   beard   _____

3. pioneers   pionears   _____

4. rain   rane   _____

5. sleap   sleep   _____

▶ Write these Spelling Words in ABC order.

| peer   year   hear   alarm   steer |

6. _____   7. _____

8. _____   9. _____

10. _____

© Harcourt

SPELLING WORDS

1. pioneers
2. cheers
3. clearing
4. hear
5. nearby
6. year
7. beard
8. reindeer
9. steer
10. peer
11. remark
12. alarm
13. sleep
14. country
15. rain

SPELLING STRATEGY

Study Steps to Learn a New Word

Use these five steps to learn new words: say, look, spell, write, check.

1. pioneers
2. cheers
3. clearing
4. hear
5. nearby
6. year
7. beard
8. reindeer
9. steer
10. peer
11. remark
12. alarm
13. sleep
14. country
15. rain

Name _____

▶ **Unscramble the Letters** Unscramble the letters to write Spelling Words.

1. ederrine _____

2. senepiro _____

3. gneclair _____

4. ebryna _____

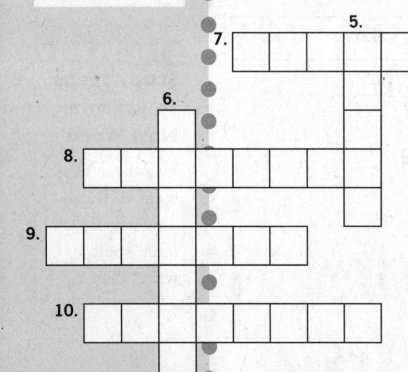

▶ **Try This!** Read the clues, and write the Spelling Words in the puzzle.

DOWN

5. a noise that warns
6. early settlers

ACROSS

7. to say something
8. animal with antlers
9. the United States
10. opening in the woods

Name _____

Words with *spr, str,* and *thr*

▶ **Finish the story. Write a Spelling Word from the box on each line.**

three	springtime	sprout	strong

In the **(1)** _____, Juan planted

(2) _____ apple seeds. They have

already started to **(3)** _____. Juan is

sure they will grow **(4)** _____.

▶ **Write a Spelling Word to complete each sentence.**

5. Ling cleared her _____ before she spoke.

6. Many _____ turn into rivers.

7. The dog jumped _____ the hoop.

▶ **Write each Spelling Word from the box on a line.**

strap	spray	ostrich

8. _____ **9.** _____ **10.** _____

© Harcourt

SPELLING WORDS

1. sprout
2. streams
3. through
4. strong
5. strap
6. springtime
7. spray
8. throat
9. three
10. ostrich
11. pioneers
12. clearing
13. air
14. different
15. light

Handwriting Tip: When you write a word, remember not to write the letters too close together or too far apart.

SPELLING WORDS

1. sprout
2. streams
3. through
4. strong
5. strap
6. springtime
7. spray
8. throat
9. three
10. ostrich
11. pioneers
12. clearing
13. air
14. different
15. light

SPELLING STRATEGY

Picture a Word and Sound It Out

To spell a word, picture it in your mind. Think about the sound each letter makes.

▶ **Find the Spelling Word that fits the clue and shape. Write the word in the shape.**

1. part of the body

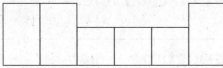

2. able to lift heavy things

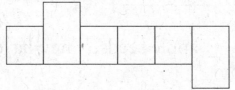

3. rhymes with *map*

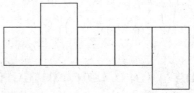

4. hit with water

5. grow

▶ **Which words do not look right? Circle the misspelled Spelling Word in each row. Then write it correctly on the line.**

6. three   strap   streems   _____

7. throat   thrugh   ostrich   _____

8. aire   spray   strap   _____

Name _____

▶ **Unscramble the Letters** Unscramble each Spelling Word.

1. metsinprgi   _____

2. iecalrgn   _____

3. cosithr   _____

4. ferfndite   _____

▶ **Picture the Word** Write Spelling Words that fit the picture clues.

5. 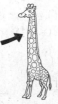   _____

6.   _____

7.   _____

8.    _____

▶ **Word Math** Add or subtract the letters shown. Write the Spelling Word.

9. hearing – h + cl = _____

10. cheers – ch + pion = _____

SPELLING WORDS

1. sprout
2. streams
3. through
4. strong
5. strap
6. springtime
7. spray
8. throat
9. three
10. ostrich
11. pioneers
12. clearing
13. air
14. different
15. light

© Harcourt

Words like *roots* and *food*

▶ **Complete the sentences. Write a Spelling Word from the box on each line.**

boot	smooth	roots	broom
moon	roof	cartoon	

1. The _____ goes around the Earth.

2. _____ are the parts of a plant that grow underground.

3. My house is covered with a _____.

4. The opposite of rough is _____.

5. Dad uses a _____ to sweep the floor.

6. A _____ is worn on the foot.

7. I watched a _____ on television.

▶ **On each line, write the Spelling Word again.**

8. spoon _____

9. scooter _____

10. food _____

© Harcourt

Name _____

▶ **Circle the correct spelling. Write the Spelling Word correctly.**

    1. broom   brom   _____

    2. bot   boot   _____

    3. spoon   spuun   _____

    4. page   paige   _____

    5. ruf   roof   _____

▶ **Use the Spelling Words in the box to complete the note.**

food	smooth	scooter	roots

Dear Ian,

    I got a new **(6)** _____! The ride is

really **(7)** _____, except when I ride

over **(8)** _____. Come try it out!

               Albert

▶ **Solve the riddle with a Spelling Word.**

    9. I am sometimes full, but I am never

        empty. I am the _____.

© Harcourt

SPELLING WORDS

1. smooth
2. roots
3. food
4. scooter
5. boot
6. broom
7. moon
8. cartoon
9. roof
10. spoon
11. springtime
12. ostrich
13. answer
14. paper
15. page

▶ **Be a Detective** Write a Spelling Word that has the shorter word in it.

1. ring _____

2. rich _____

3. an _____

4. ape _____

▶ **Word Change** Change the underlined letter or letters to make a Spelling Word. Write the Spelling Word.

5. sco<u>u</u>ter _____

6. <u>har</u>poon _____

7. p<u>i</u>per _____

8. an<u>ch</u>or _____

▶ **Think About It** Which two Spelling Words rhyme with *moon*? Write them.

9. _____   10. _____

© Harcourt

Name_____

Words with *gn, kn,* and *wr*

▶ Label each picture. Write a Spelling Word from the box on each line.

write	sign	wrist

1. _____

2. _____

3. _____

▶ **Dictionary** Write these Spelling Words in ABC order.

knight	gnat	knock	writer

4. _____ 5. _____

6. _____ 7. _____

▶ Write each Spelling Word from the box on a line.

knew	unknown

8. _____ 9. _____

1. knock
2. knew
3. knight
4. wrong
5. write
6. sign
7. gnat
8. wrist
9. unknown
10. writer
11. scooter
12. cartoon
13. dark
14. front
15. past

Handwriting Tip: When you write the letter *n*, make the straight line first. Start at the midline.

n

SPELLING WORDS

1. knock
2. knew
3. knight
4. wrong
5. write
6. sign
7. gnat
8. wrist
9. unknown
10. writer
11. scooter
12. cartoon
13. dark
14. front
15. past

SPELLING STRATEGY

Guess and Check

If you are unsure about a spelling, take a guess and see if it looks right. Then check your guess.

▶ **Add the letters *kn* or *wr* before each ending. Then write the Spelling Word.**

1. ____ ____ite _____

2. ____ ____ist _____

3. ____ ____ew _____

4. ____ ____ong _____

5. ____ ____ock _____

▶ **Which words do not look right? Circle the misspelled Spelling Word in each row. Then write it correctly on the line.**

6. frount   knock   write   _____

7. wrong   scooter   darck   _____

8. signe   knight   wrist   _____

9. cartoon   passt   knew   _____

10. unknown   ngat   writer   _____

© Harcourt

Name _____

▶ **Rhymes** Find a Spelling Word that rhymes with the underlined word and makes sense in the sentence. Write the word on the line.

SPELLING WORDS

1. knock
2. knew
3. knight
4. wrong
5. write
6. sign
7. gnat
8. wrist
9. unknown
10. writer
11. scooter
12. cartoon
13. dark
14. front
15. past

1. A <u>twist</u> of the _____ hurts!

2. What was once _____ will now be <u>shown</u>.

3. The _____ wore <u>white</u>.

4. That _____ is also a <u>firefighter</u>.

5. I _____ the <u>stew</u> would be good.

6. That <u>song</u> sounds all _____.

▶ Use the code to spell Spelling Words.

1 = n	2 = c	3 = w	4 = t	5 = k
6 = e	7 = u	8 = p	9 = o	10 = r
11 = i	12 = f	13 = s	14 = a	

7. 7-1-5-1-9-3-1   _____

8. 2-14-10-4-9-9-1   _____

9. 13-2-9-9-4-6-10   _____

10. 5-1-9-2-5   _____

© Harcourt

Words That End with -s, -es, and -ies

▶ Finish the advertisement. Write a Spelling Word from the box on each line.

beauties	babies	cities	duties
skies	pennies	hobbies	

VISIT OUR TOWN THIS FALL

Fall is the time to see the **(1)** _____ of our town. The **(2)** _____ are blue and clear. Visitors throw **(3)** _____ into sparkling fountains and try new **(4)** _____. Mothers stroll in the parks with their

(5) _____. Workers perform their

(6) _____ to keep things neat. Ours is

one of the best **(7)** _____ to visit in fall!

▶ On each line, write the Spelling Word again.

8. bodies _____ 9. cries _____

10. copies _____

© Harcourt

▶ **Add the ending. Write the Spelling Word.**

1. baby (es) _____

2. duty (es) _____

3. body (es) _____

4. sky (es) _____

5. cry (es) _____

▶ **Circle the word that is correct. Then write the Spelling Word on the line.**

6. My grandmother lives high on a (**hil, hill**). _____

7. I got a (**drink, drinck**) from the water fountain. _____

8. Did you see the stop (**signe, sign**)? _____

9. Look both ways before you cross the (**road, raod**). _____

SPELLING WORDS

1. beauties
2. babies
3. cities
4. duties
5. bodies
6. skies
7. copies
8. cries
9. pennies
10. hobbies
11. sign
12. unknown
13. drink
14. hill
15. road

SPELLING STRATEGY

Spelling Patterns

Remember the pattern when adding -*es* to words with similar endings.

© Harcourt

SPELLING WORDS

1. beauties
2. babies
3. cities
4. duties
5. bodies
6. skies
7. copies
8. cries
9. pennies
10. hobbies
11. sign
12. unknown
13. drink
14. hill
15. road

▶ **Ask Me a Question** Write a Spelling Word to answer each question.

What are jobs to do?   1. _____

What are young children?   2. _____

What are one-cent coins?   3. _____

Where do many people live?   4. _____

What are things that look

exactly alike?   5. _____

▶ **Word Hunt** Circle five Spelling Words in the puzzle. Then write them.

6. _____

7. _____

8. _____

9. _____

10. _____

m	b	o	d	i	e	s
f	e	p	a	b	k	h
q	a	d	j	l	w	o
d	u	t	i	e	s	b
e	t	k	r	h	e	b
c	i	t	i	e	s	i
p	e	n	d	k	c	e
o	s	l	t	f	a	s

© Harcourt

Practice Test

A. Read each sentence. Find the correctly spelled word that completes the sentence. Fill in the circle in front of that word.

Example: The man has a long _____ .

   ⊂⊃ beerd   ⬤ beard   ⊂⊃ baerd

1. Jen has a shiny new _____ .

   ⊂⊃ scooter   ⊂⊃ scouter   ⊂⊃ scootter

2. The author of the poem is _____ .

   ⊂⊃ unown   ⊂⊃ unknown   ⊂⊃ unknoon

3. Five _____ make a nickel.

   ⊂⊃ pennies   ⊂⊃ penies   ⊂⊃ pennyes

4. The _____ cannot fly.

   ⊂⊃ ostich   ⊂⊃ ostrick   ⊂⊃ ostrich

5. Do you have any _____ ?

   ⊂⊃ hobies   ⊂⊃ hobbies   ⊂⊃ hobbyes

6. In the _____ , flowers bloom.

   ⊂⊃ springtime   ⊂⊃ spingtime   ⊂⊃ stringtime

7. The two _____ are playing together.

   ⊂⊃ babies   ⊂⊃ babys   ⊂⊃ babbies

© Harcourt

Name_____

B. Read each sentence. Is the spelling of the underlined word correct or incorrect? Fill in the circle in front of your answer.

Example: I'm in second grade this <u>yere</u>.

    ○ correct   ● incorrect

1. <u>Reindeer</u> live where it is cold.

    ○ correct   ○ incorrect

2. The park's roses are <u>beeuties</u>.

    ○ correct   ○ incorrect

3. She is my favorite <u>riter</u>.

    ○ correct   ○ incorrect

4. Let's have a picnic in this <u>clearing</u>.

    ○ correct   ○ incorrect

5. Zebras have striped <u>bodys</u>.

    ○ correct   ○ incorrect

6. This <u>cartoon</u> is very funny.

    ○ correct   ○ incorrect

7. We ran home <u>thrugh</u> the rain.

    ○ correct   ○ incorrect

8. My cousin lives <u>neerby</u>.

    ○ correct   ○ incorrect

9. The teacher made <u>copies</u> of the test.

    ○ correct   ○ incorrect

10. These <u>streams</u> flow into the sea.

    ○ correct   ○ incorrect

© Harcourt

Name _____

Words with *ou* and *ow*

▶ Use Spelling Words from the box to finish the story.

how	out	house
found	sound	now	without

One day, my cat wasn't in my

(1) _____ . I panicked! Then I heard a

(2) _____ . I **(3)** _____ him in the

shed. I don't know **(4)** _____ he got

there. **(5)** _____ that he is back, I'm

not letting him **(6)** _____ of my sight

again. I don't know what I'd do

(7) _____ him!

▶ On each line, write the Spelling Word again.

8. around _____   **9.** brow _____

10. mouth _____

SPELLING WORDS

1. how
2. mouth
3. out
4. house
5. without
6. found
7. around
8. sound
9. now
10. brow
11. beauties
12. skies
13. started
14. mean
15. cow

Handwriting Tip: When you write the letter *o*, be sure to close the letter completely so your *o* does not look like a *c*.

© Harcourt

1. how
2. mouth
3. out
4. house
5. without
6. found
7. around
8. sound
9. now
10. brow
11. beauties
12. skies
13. started
14. mean
15. cow

Sounds and Letters

Some vowel sounds can be spelled different ways. Think about the different ways a word can be spelled.

Name _____

▶ **Circle the pair of letters that correctly spell the vowel sound in each Spelling Word. Then write the Spelling Word on the line.**

1. withowt   without   _____

2. house   howse   _____

3. brow   brou   _____

4. arownd   around   _____

5. hou   how   _____

▶ **Find the Spelling Word that fits the clue and shape. Write the word in the shape.**

6. at this moment

7. located

8. part of the face

9. noise

10. not in

© Harcourt

Name_____

1. how
2. mouth
3. out
4. house
5. without
6. found
7. around
8. sound
9. now
10. brow
11. beauties
12. skies
13. started
14. mean
15. cow

▶ **Rhymes** Find the Spelling Word that rhymes with the underlined word and makes sense in the sentence.

1. Wow! Look at the white _____.

2. This bird flies only in blue _____.

3. The _____ of the river is south.

▶ **Try This!** Read the clues, and write the Spelling Words in the puzzle.

DOWN

4. not nice
6. surrounding
8. in what way
10. place to live

ACROSS

5. began
7. not having
9. bright, blue _____

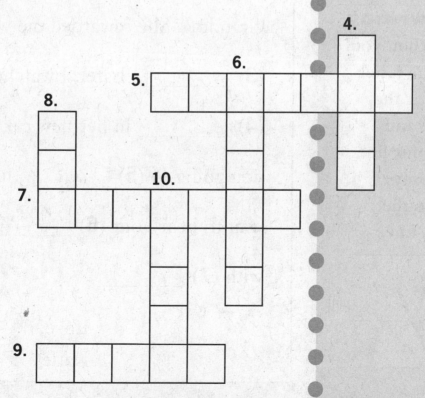

© Harcourt

1. voices
2. cowboys
3. toy
4. enjoyment
5. oil
6. point
7. join
8. soil
9. joy
10. coin
11. around
12. without
13. fire
14. train
15. wait

Handwriting Tip: When you write the letter *y*, start at the midline and bring your line all the way down to the bottom line.

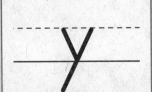

Name _____

Words with *oi* and *oy*

▶ Use Spelling Words from the box to finish the letter.

| join   soil   coin   oil   joy   point   voices |

Dear Mom and Dad,

I am having fun at Grandma's house. Today we picked flowers that grew in her garden. I was careful not to get

(1) _____ on my clean, white shoes. I took care to **(2)** _____ that out to Grandma. She rewarded me with a

(3) _____! Later, I watched as she put

(4) _____ in her new car. When are you going to **(5)** _____ us here? I can't wait to hear your **(6)** _____. I am filled with **(7)** _____.

Love,
Katie

© Harcourt

Name _____

▶ **Find the Spelling Word that rhymes with the underlined word and makes sense.**

1. The rancher <u>employs</u> several

   _____.

2. _____ to the <u>joint</u> that squeaks.

3. The miners found <u>oil</u> deep beneath

   _____.

4. Please don't <u>shout</u>. I won't leave

   _____ it.

5. Our dog <u>rejoices</u> when he hears our

   _____.

6. The baby's loud _____ is starting
   to <u>annoy</u> me.

▶ **Add vowels to complete the Spelling Word. Then write the whole word.**

7. c _____ n   _____

8. ____ nj _____ m ____ nt

   _____

SPELLING WORDS

1. voices
2. cowboys
3. toy
4. enjoyment
5. oil
6. point
7. join
8. soil
9. joy
10. coin
11. around
12. without
13. fire
14. train
15. wait

SPELLING
STRATEGY
Rhyming Words

Try using the same letter pattern of a word that rhymes with the word you want to spell.

© Harcourt

1. voices
2. cowboys
3. toy
4. enjoyment
5. oil
6. point
7. join
8. soil
9. joy
10. coin
11. around
12. without
13. fire
14. train
15. wait

Name _____

Fun with Words

▶ Write the Spelling Word for each picture.

1. _____   2. _____

3. _____   4. _____

▶ **Word Opposites** Read each word. Write the Spelling Word that has the opposite meaning.

5. sorrow   _____

6. silence   _____

7. quit   _____

8. boredom   _____

▶ **Word Scramble** Unscramble the Spelling Words. (Hint: Find *oy* first.)

9. owysocb   _____

10. tomeenynj   _____

© Harcourt

Name _____

Words with *oo* and *ue*

▶ **Complete the sentences with these Spelling Words.**

zoo	room	blue
too	due	noontime	rooftop

1. The sky is _____.

2. Can I come, _____?

3. This _____ has a big window.

4. When is our homework _____?

5. Animals live at the _____.

6. I eat my lunch at _____.

7. The chimney is on the _____ of my house.

▶ **On each line, write the Spelling Word again.**

8. glue _____   9. clue _____

10. true _____

SPELLING WORDS

1. blue
2. too
3. glue
4. zoo
5. room
6. clue
7. due
8. rooftop
9. true
10. noontime
11. cowboys
12. voices
13. letter
14. sea
15. won't

Handwriting Tip:
When writing the letter *u*, be sure to curve the bottom line so your *u* does not look like a *v*.

U

1. blue
2. too
3. glue
4. zoo
5. room
6. clue
7. due
8. rooftop
9. true
10. noontime
11. cowboys
12. voices
13. letter
14. sea
15. won't

Name _____

▶ **Proofread the postcard. Circle the incorrect words. Then write the Spelling Words correctly.**

Dear Gabriel,

Today I went to the zou. I saw a blou parrot. It flew around until noontyme, then went right up on the ruftop. It's troo! I think it escaped. I don't have a clew where it is now. Maybe it went to a secret rume. Isn't that cool?

Jason

1. _____   2. _____

3. _____   4. _____

5. _____   6. _____

7. _____

▶ **Which words do not look right? Circle the misspelled Spelling Word in each row. Then write it correctly on the line.**

8. letter   deu   voices   _____

9. zoo   sea   nountime   _____

10. coyboys   clue   won't   _____

© Harcourt

Name _____

▶ **Dictionary** Write these four Spelling Words in ABC order.

won't	too	cowboys	sea

1. _____   2. _____

3. _____   4. _____

▶ **Word Find** Find four Spelling Words in the puzzle and circle them. Write these words on the lines.

5. _____   6. _____

7. _____   8. _____

```
l z d g u a w b
a r o o f t o p
n o o n t i m e
g o l e t t e r
u m h s n p r n
```

▶ **Try This!** Write the Spelling Words that make the word math sentence true.

9. _____ $- g + b =$ **10.** _____

SPELLING WORDS

1. blue
2. too
3. glue
4. zoo
5. room
6. clue
7. due
8. rooftop
9. true
10. noontime
11. cowboys
12. voices
13. letter
14. sea
15. won't

© Harcourt

1. wife
2. wives
3. leaf
4. leaves
5. elf
6. elves
7. shelf
8. shelves
9. life
10. lives
11. rooftop
12. true
13. bone
14. draw
15. whose

Handwriting Tip: When you make your letters, be sure they are even and dark enough to read.

_____

- - - S - - -

Name _____

Plurals with -es

▶ Write a Spelling Word for each picture. Circle the endings: *f, fe,* or *ves*

1.  _____

2. _____

3. _____

▶ Write two Spelling Words that rhyme with each word. Underline the *f, fe,* or *ves.*

4. hives _____

   _____

5. knife _____

   _____

▶ Write each Spelling Word from the box on a line.

elves	leaves	shelves

6. _____   7. _____

8. _____

© Harcourt

▶ **ABC Order** Write the Spelling Words in ABC order. Circle the word that means more than one.

wives	shelf	leaf	bone

1. _____   2. _____

3. _____   4. _____

▶ **Fun with Words** Unscramble the letters to write Spelling Words on the lines.

fel	fwei	awdr	uetr	vsaeel	sewho

5. _____   6. _____

7. _____   8. _____

9. _____   10. _____

© Harcourt

SPELLING WORDS

1. wife
2. wives
3. leaf
4. leaves
5. elf
6. elves
7. shelf
8. shelves
9. life
10. lives
11. rooftop
12. true
13. bone
14. draw
15. whose

SPELLING STRATEGY

Pay attention to word endings. Did you make any needed spelling change before adding -s or -es to each word?

1. wife
2. wives
3. leaf
4. leaves
5. elf
6. elves
7. shelf
8. shelves
9. life
10. lives
11. rooftop
12. true
13. bone
14. draw
15. whose

Name _____

▶ **Use the clues. Add three letters. Then write the Spelling Word.**

1. Dogs eat me as a treat. I'm a

b____ ____ ____.

2. You may put books on me.

I'm sh____ ____ve____.

3. I protect your house from the rain, snow, wind, and hail. I'm

the ro____ ____ ____op.

4. We wear pointy shoes and make you

laugh. We're el____ ____ ____.

5. We fall from the trees in autumn.

We're l____ ____ ____es.

▶ **Word Math** Write the Spelling Words.

6. wive + s = _____

7. roof + top = _____

8. leaf - f + ves = _____

9. live - ve + fe = _____

Name _____

Words that end with
-ing and -ly

▶ Use Spelling Words to finish the letter.

| doing | swimming | slowly |
| eating | starting | actually | taking |

Dear Grandma,

I am **(1)** _____ lots of things at

camp! I'm **(2)** _____ sailing lessons,

and I'm **(3)** _____ getting better.

Next week I'll be **(4)** _____ a class

in **(5)** _____. Thank you for the

cookies. I have enjoyed **(6)** _____

and sharing them.

                              Love,
                              Dru

▶ On each line, write the Spelling Word again.

7. standing _____

8. freezing _____

SPELLING WORDS

1. completely
2. actually
3. doing
4. taking
5. swimming
6. eating
7. slowly
8. starting
9. standing
10. freezing
11. leaf
12. leaves
13. important
14. nothing
15. dinner

Handwriting Tip: When you write the letter g, close the circle completely, and hook the tail to the left so that it does not look like a q.

_____

g

1. completely
2. actually
3. doing
4. taking
5. swimming
6. eating
7. slowly
8. starting
9. standing
10. freezing
11. leaf
12. leaves
13. important
14. nothing
15. dinner

Name _____

▶ **Add the ending to each word. Write the Spelling Word.**

1. actual (ly) _____

2. take (ing) _____

3. leave (s) _____

4. slow (ly) _____

5. start (ing) _____

▶ **Proofread the sentences. Circle the incorrect Spelling Words. Write them correctly on the lines.**

6. I saw Joe standng at the bus stop.

_____

7. He looked completly frozen.

_____

8. I asked him what he was doeing there.

_____

9. At first he said noting. _____

10. Then he said he was going to his

swiming lesson. _____

© Harcourt

Name_____

▶ **Use the clues. Write the Spelling Word.**

1. totally _____

2. very cold _____

3. in fact _____

4. the opposite of quickly _____

5. meal at the end of the day _____

▶ **Use the code to make the Spelling Words.**

1 = e	2 = t	3 = g	4 = r	5 = w
6 = i	7 = a	8 = d	9 = n	10 = m
11 = s	12 = o	13 = p	14 = l	15 = f

6. 6-10-13-12-4-2-7-9-2 _____

7. 1-7-2-6-9-3 _____

8. 11-2-7-9-8-6-9-3 _____

9. 14-1-7-15 _____

10. 11-5-6-10-10-6-9-3 _____

© Harcourt

SPELLING WORDS

1. completely
2. actually
3. doing
4. taking
5. swimming
6. eating
7. slowly
8. starting
9. standing
10. freezing
11. leaf
12. leaves
13. important
14. nothing
15. dinner

Practice Test

A. Read each sentence. Find the correctly spelled word that completes the sentence. Fill in the circle in front of that word.

Example: I chew my meat _____.
    ◯ slowlie   ◯ slowaly   ━ slowly

1. They say cats have nine _____.
    ◯ lives   ◯ lifes   ◯ livs

2. The singers have nice _____.
    ◯ voces   ◯ voices   ◯ voyces

3. I left home _____ my lunch.
    ◯ withot   ◯ witout   ◯ without

4. I am _____ dance class next week.
    ◯ staring   ◯ startting   ◯ starting

5. We took a walk _____ the garden.
    ◯ around   ◯ arownd   ◯ aroond

6. My _____ is red from juice.
    ◯ mouth   ◯ mounth   ◯ mowth

7. I am _____ my homework now.
    ◯ duing   ◯ dewing   ◯ doing

B. Read each sentence. Find the underlined Spelling Word that is spelled correctly. Fill in the circle below it.

Example: It is <u>importat</u> to be on time for <u>dinner</u>.

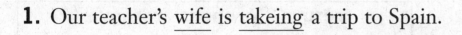

1. Our teacher's <u>wife</u> is <u>takeing</u> a trip to Spain.
   ◯ ◯

2. In this story, <u>elfs</u> live under a <u>leaf</u>.
   ◯ ◯

3. I <u>completeley</u> forgot the book was <u>due</u>.
   ◯ ◯

4. My <u>roum</u> is <u>actually</u> not very messy.
   ◯ ◯

5. The <u>cowboys</u> <u>fownd</u> the lost calf.
   ◯ ◯

6. Jessie has a great <u>enjoiment</u> of <u>life</u>.
   ◯ ◯

7. Is it <u>true</u> you're coming <u>tou</u>?
   ◯ ◯

8. The snail <u>slowly</u> dug into the <u>soile</u>.
   ◯ ◯

9. <u>Hou</u> did they get on the <u>rooftop</u>?
   ◯ ◯

10. This <u>howse</u> needs more <u>shelves</u>.
    ◯ ◯

SPELLING WORDS

1. remove
2. return
3. recycle
4. replace
5. recall
6. preheat
7. prepay
8. preschool
9. preview
10. prefix
11. swimming
12. doing
13. maybe
14. near
15. park

Handwriting Tip: When you write a *p*, remember that the straight line goes on the left and extends below the bottom line.

Words That Begin with *re-* and *pre-*

▶ **Complete the sentences. Write a Spelling Word from the box on each line.**

return	preheat	remove
preview	preschool	recycle	recall

1. My little sister goes to _____.

2. I don't _____ what the teacher said.

3. _____ the oven before putting in the cake.

4. Let's _____ this junk from the attic.

5. I saw a _____ of that movie last week.

6. I must _____ this library book.

7. We can _____ these bottles and cans.

▶ **Write each Spelling Word from the box on the line.**

prepay	prefix	replace

8. _____   9. _____   10. _____

© Harcourt

Name _____

► **Add the prefix to each word. Write the Spelling Word.**

1. (pre) pay   _____

2. (re) cycle   _____

3. (re) move   _____

4. (pre) view   _____

5. (pre) school   _____

► **Circle the correct spelling of each Spelling Word. Then write the word correctly on the line.**

6. neer   near   _____

7. replace   replase   _____

8. park   parck   _____

9. mabee   maybe   _____

10. swimming   swiming   _____

SPELLING WORDS

1. remove
2. return
3. recycle
4. replace
5. recall
6. preheat
7. prepay
8. preschool
9. preview
10. prefix
11. swimming
12. doing
13. maybe
14. near
15. park

SPELLING STRATEGY

Beginnings

To spell words with prefixes, think of the spelling of the base word, then add the prefix at the beginning.

SPELLING WORDS

1. remove
2. return
3. recycle
4. replace
5. recall
6. preheat
7. prepay
8. preschool
9. preview
10. prefix
11. swimming
12. doing
13. maybe
14. near
15. park

▶ **Word Change** Change the underlined letter or letters to make a Spelling Word.

1. rec<u>oi</u>l _____   2. ret<u>i</u>re _____

3. rem<u>o</u>te _____   4. d<u>r</u>ink _____

5. re<u>t</u>race _____   6. pret<u>e</u>nd _____

▶ **Word Shapes** Write a Spelling Word in each word shape. Then write the word on the line.

7. _____

8. _____

9. _____

10. _____

© Harcourt

Name _____

Contractions

▶ Write the Spelling Word that is the contraction for each pair of words.

1. we will   _____

2. it is   _____

3. should not   _____

4. is not   _____

5. do not   _____

6. can not   _____

7. that is   _____

8. I will   _____

9. you will   _____

10. they will   _____

© Harcourt

SPELLING WORDS

1. we'll
2. I'll
3. you'll
4. they'll
5. don't
6. can't
7. isn't
8. it's
9. that's
10. shouldn't
11. preheat
12. recycle
13. shop
14. surprise
15. kittens

Handwriting Tip: When you write a tall letter like *l*, remember that it should touch the top line.

SPELLING WORDS

1. we'll
2. I'll
3. you'll
4. they'll
5. don't
6. can't
7. isn't
8. it's
9. that's
10. shouldn't
11. preheat
12. recycle
13. shop
14. surprise
15. kittens

SPELLING STRATEGY

Patterns with Contractions

Remember contractions that use *will*, *not*, and *is* are always made the same way (*'ll*, *n't*, and *'s*).

▶ **Proofread the list. Circle each word that is not correct. Write the four incorrect Spelling Words correctly.**

don't	shopp	kittens
is'nt	we'll	ile
that's	shudn't	it's

1. _____

2. _____

3. _____

4. _____

▶ **Circle two words that make a contraction. Write the Spelling Word.**

5. they   do   not   _____

6. can   not   you   _____

7. we   can   will   _____

8. you   will   do   _____

9. it   is   we   _____

10. do   they   will   _____

SPELLING PRACTICE BOOK   LESSON 2

© Harcourt

Name _____

▶ **Mixed-Up Words** Unscramble the letters to write Spelling Words.

1. cryelec   _____

2. st'aht   _____

3. rpehtae   _____

4. st'in   _____

5. sspreiur   _____

6. setntik   _____

▶ **What's Missing?** Write the Spelling Words. Put the apostrophe where it belongs.

7. youll   _____

8. theyll   _____

9. cant   _____

10. dont   _____

SPELLING WORDS
1. we'll
2. I'll
3. you'll
4. they'll
5. don't
6. can't
7. isn't
8. it's
9. that's
10. shouldn't
11. preheat
12. recycle
13. shop
14. surprise
15. kittens

1. new
2. crew
3. stew
4. grew
5. threw
6. bruise
7. fruit
8. pursuit
9. juice
10. recruit
11. you'll
12. shouldn't
13. church
14. windows
15. sisters

Handwriting Tip: When you write short letters like *e*, *u*, and *w*, make sure they sit on the bottom line and touch the midline.

Name _____

Words with *ew* and *ui*

▶ Complete the poster. Write a Spelling Word from the box on each line.

juice	fruit	stew	recruit
	grew	new	crew

JOIN THE COOKING CLUB

Come join our **(1)** _____! The cooking

club wants to **(2)** _____ some

(3) _____ members. Last year we

(4) _____ our own garden. We pressed

(5) _____ into yummy **(6)** _____.
We also made a hot and hearty

(7) _____ and many other treats. We
hope to see you at our first meeting!

▶ Write a Spelling Word from the box on each line.

threw	bruise	pursuit

8. _____   9. _____

10. _____

© Harcourt

Name _____

► **Circle the correct spelling of each Spelling Word. Then write the word on the line.**

1. stoo   stew   _____

2. you'll   youl   _____

3. church   cherch   _____

4. nu   new   _____

► **Use Spelling Words to complete each sentence. Write the correct spelling of each word.**

The boat's **(5) (crue, crew)** _____ went

in **(6) (pursuit, pursewt)** _____ of fish.

The apple seeds Johnny **(7) (threu, threw)**

_____ on the ground soon **(8) (grew,**

groo) _____ into apple trees.

I don't like **(9) (fruit, frewt)** _____ but

I do like **(10) (joose, juice)** _____ .

© Harcourt

LESSON 3   **SPELLING PRACTICE BOOK**   **85**

SPELLING WORDS

1. new
2. crew
3. stew
4. grew
5. threw
6. bruise
7. fruit
8. pursuit
9. juice
10. recruit
11. you'll
12. shouldn't
13. church
14. windows
15. sisters

SPELLING STRATEGY

Try Different Spellings

Remember that the *oo* sound can be spelled different ways. Try different spellings if you are not sure.

SPELLING WORDS

1. new
2. crew
3. stew
4. grew
5. threw
6. bruise
7. fruit
8. pursuit
9. juice
10. recruit
11. you'll
12. shouldn't
13. church
14. windows
15. sisters

▶ **Fun with Words** Write the Spelling Word that makes sense in the sentence.

1. You _____ ride your bike without a helmet.

2. Carlos opened all the _____ to let in the fresh air.

3. Hannah has three _____ and one brother.

4. Let's _____ some helpers.

5. If you fall, you might get a _____.

▶ Use the code to make Spelling Words.

1 = o	2 = d	3 = s	4 = u	5 = n
6 = i	7 = w	8 = c	9 = l	10 = r
11 = e	12 = t	13 = f	14 = p	

6. 10-11-8-10-4-6-12 _____

7. 13-10-4-6-12 _____

8. 7-6-5-2-1-7-3 _____

9. 3-6-3-12-11-10-3 _____

10. 14-4-10-3-4-6-12 _____

© Harcourt

Name _____

Words with *gh* and *ph*

▶ **Finish the sentences. Write a Spelling Word from the box on each line.**

telephone	rough	tough	enough
graph	photo	paragraph	

1. We made a bar _____ in math class.

2. It contains a few sentences. It is a

    _____.

3. It is hard to do. It is _____.

4. The road has holes in it. It is a

    _____ road.

5. I ate a lot of food. I had more than

    _____.

6. We took a picture. Here is the

    _____.

7. I called my friend. We talked on the

    _____.

SPELLING WORDS

1. paragraph
2. petroglyphs
3. photo
4. telephone
5. graph
6. laugh
7. cough
8. rough
9. enough
10. tough
11. pursuit
12. recruit
13. birthday
14. buy
15. dance

Handwriting Tip: When you write the letter g, make the tail curve to the left.

g

SPELLING WORDS

1. paragraph
2. petroglyphs
3. photo
4. telephone
5. graph
6. laugh
7. cough
8. rough
9. enough
10. tough
11. pursuit
12. recruit
13. birthday
14. buy
15. dance

SPELLING STRATEGY

Guess and Check

If you are unsure of a spelling, take a guess. Then check your spelling with a dictionary.

▶ **Proofread the sentences. Circle the words that are misspelled. Write the Spelling Words correctly on the lines.**

1. Don't make me laff. _____

2. Hang up the telefone. _____

3. We played in a tuff game today. _____

4. I had a bad couph last week. _____

5. Look at the beautiful petrogliphs.

_____

▶ **Dictionary** Write these Spelling Words in ABC order.

buy   dance   graph   rough   enough

6. _____   7. _____

8. _____   9. _____

10. _____

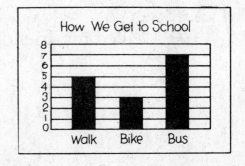

How We Get to School

▶ **Word Scramble** Unscramble each Spelling Word. Write the words.

1. agarpahrp _____

2. psirutu _____

3. topoh _____

4. sportypeghl _____

5. hbryaitd _____

6. uticerr _____

▶ Use the code to make Spelling Words.

1 = a	2 = u	3 = g	4 = h	5 = o
6 = i	7 = r	8 = b	9 = e	10 = n
11 = p	12 = c	13 = t	14 = d	15 = y

7. 7-9-12-7-2-6-13 _____

8. 8-6-7-13-4-14-1-15 _____

9. 11-1-7-1-3-7-1-11-4 _____

10. 9-10-5-2-3-4 _____

SPELLING WORDS

1. paragraph
2. petroglyphs
3. photo
4. telephone
5. graph
6. laugh
7. cough
8. rough
9. enough
10. tough
11. pursuit
12. recruit
13. birthday
14. buy
15. dance

© Harcourt

SPELLING WORDS

1. taller
2. tallest
3. fresher
4. freshest
5. smaller
6. smallest
7. smarter
8. smartest
9. happier
10. happiest
11. paragraph
12. telephone
13. lion
14. oil
15. men

Words That End with -er and -est

▶ Complete the letter. Write a Spelling Word from the box on each line.

freshest	happier	smaller
	taller	tallest

Dear Aunt Linda,

I have grown a lot (1) _____ since you

were here. I think I am the (2) _____

boy in class now! Even my friend Pedro is

(3) _____ than me now. I hope you are

coming to visit soon. I am always

(4) _____ when you are here, and you

bring the (5) _____ fruit from Florida.
I can't wait to see you!

Love,

Brian

Handwriting Tip: When you write the letter *t*, cross it at the midline, like this:

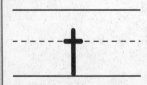

▶ Circle the correct spelling. Write the Spelling Word correctly.

6. smartst   smartest   _____

7. fresher   freshre   _____

© Harcourt

Name _____

▶ **Add the ending to each word. Write the Spelling Word.**

1. fresh (est) _____

2. smart (er) _____

3. happy (er) _____

4. happy (est) _____

5. fresh (er) _____

6. smart (est) _____

▶ **Look at the pictures. Write the Spelling Word that makes each sentence true.**

7. Trudy is _____ than Judy.

8. Judy is the _____ of the children.

9. Trudy is _____ than Rudy.

10. Rudy is the _____ of the three.

Rudy   Trudy   Judy

© Harcourt

SPELLING WORDS

1. taller
2. tallest
3. fresher
4. freshest
5. smaller
6. smallest
7. smarter
8. smartest
9. happier
10. happiest
11. paragraph
12. telephone
13. lion
14. oil
15. men

SPELLING
STRATEGY
Endings

Remember that words ending with *-er* compare two things, and words ending with *-est* compare more than two.

SPELLING WORDS

1. taller
2. tallest
3. fresher
4. freshest
5. smaller
6. smallest
7. smarter
8. smartest
9. happier
10. happiest
11. paragraph
12. telephone
13. lion
14. oil
15. men

▶ **Word Shapes** Write the Spelling Word that matches the clue and fits in the shape.

1. most joyful

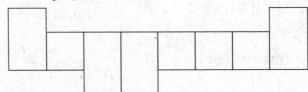

2. more recently picked

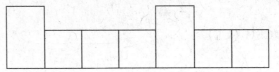

3. littler

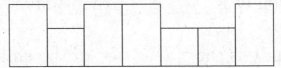

4. measuring the highest

▶ **Word Search** Circle five Spelling Words. Then write the words.

```
h f j t a d y t f
u o i l e n f e k
i f n k s l e l e
u e n b o w b e s
p a r a g r a p h
s o l f j e n h h
d m x s x z t o w
u e x d l i o n p
d n k d h u e e t
```

5. _____   6. _____

7. _____   8. _____

9. _____

© Harcourt

Practice Test

A. Read each sentence. Find the correctly spelled word that completes each sentence. Fill in the circle in front of that word.

Example: I usually _____ when I have a cold.

    ◯ couff   ◯ couhg   ⬤ cough

1. She said _____ be a little late.

    ◯ theill   ◯ theyll   ◯ they'll

2. Did you get _____ to eat?

    ◯ enouph   ◯ enough   ◯ enouh

3. This is just a _____ of the movie.

    ◯ preveew   ◯ preview   ◯ preeview

4. These _____ are very old.

    ◯ petroglyfs   ◯ petrogliphs   ◯ petroglyphs

5. People _____ litter.

    ◯ shouldn't   ◯ shouldnot   ◯ shoudn't

6. People should _____ instead.

    ◯ recicle   ◯ recycle   ◯ reecycle

7. Who is _____, you or Frank?

    ◯ talller   ◯ taler   ◯ taller

Name _____

B. Read each sentence. Decide if the spelling of the underlined word is correct. Fill in the circle in front of your answer.

Example: Today is my berthday!

   ○ correct   ● incorrect

1. We ran off in pursoot of our dog.

   ○ correct   ○ incorrect

2. My aunt teaches preschool.

   ○ correct   ○ incorrect

3. Pick up the telefone.

   ○ correct   ○ incorrect

4. Today was the happyest day of my life!

   ○ correct   ○ incorrect

5. Jason grew a lot last year.

   ○ correct   ○ incorrect

6. Maggie is'nt coming to the party.

   ○ correct   ○ incorrect

7. I do not think he is smarter than you.

   ○ correct   ○ incorrect

8. Write a paragraph about your trip.

   ○ correct   ○ incorrect

9. Remouv your books from your desks.

   ○ correct   ○ incorrect

10. That's a funny story.

   ○ correct   ○ incorrect

© Harcourt

Name_____

Words with *air* and *are*

▶ Write a Spelling Word from the box on each line.

airplanes	pair	scare	careful
rare	airport	chair	

A museum director who went to the

(1) _____ got quite a **(2)** _____

yesterday. He was supposed to pick up two

very **(3)** _____ artworks for the

museum, but they were not at the right

place. After checking inside several

(4) _____, he found the **(5)** _____

of paintings sitting on a **(6)** _____ in

the Lost and Found! You can never be too

(7) _____ when you label your bags.

▶ On each line, write the Spelling Word again.

8. dare _____   **9.** hair _____

10. share _____

© Harcourt

SPELLING WORDS

1. airport
2. airplanes
3. chair
4. careful
5. dare
6. share
7. rare
8. scare
9. hair
10. pair
11. tallest
12. happier
13. boat
14. city
15. morning

Handwriting Tip: Remember that when writing an *a*, make sure to close the circle entirely.

_____

- - - - - - -

a

1. airport
2. airplanes
3. chair
4. careful
5. dare
6. share
7. rare
8. scare
9. hair
10. pair
11. tallest
12. happier
13. boat
14. city
15. morning

SPELLING
STRATEGY
Use the
Dictionary
Remember to
use the
dictionary
whenever you
are unsure
about a spelling.

Name _____

▶ **Circle the misspelled Spelling Word in each row. Then write it correctly on the line.**

1. rair   dare   scare _____

2. chair   haire   airport _____

3. tallest   shaire   pair _____

▶ **Proofread the sentences. Circle the Spelling Words that are misspelled. Write them correctly on the lines.**

4. I went to a new shoe store on a dair.

    _____

5. I sat on a broken chare. _____

6. I had quite a scair. _____

7. Next time I will be more cairful.

    _____

8. The salesperson gave me a free pare of

    shoelaces. _____

▶ **Unscramble the letters to write Spelling Words.**

9. atob _____   10. tyic _____

© Harcourt

Name_____

► **Use the clues. Add three letters. Then write the Spelling Word.**

1. When the sun rises, it is

   mo____ ____ ____ng. _____

2. These machines fly. They are

   a____ ____ ____lanes. _____

3. When I am cautious, I am

   c____ ____ ____ful. _____

4. I am more joyful. I am

   hap____ ____ ____r. _____

5. When we fly, we leave from the

   ____ ____ ____port. _____

► **Fun with Words** Find five Spelling Words in the puzzle. Circle each one. Then write the words on the lines.

6. _____   7. _____

8. _____   9. _____

10. _____

SPELLING WORDS

1. airport
2. airplanes
3. chair
4. careful
5. dare
6. share
7. rare
8. scare
9. hair
10. pair
11. tallest
12. happier
13. boat
14. city
15. morning

a	i	r	p	l	a	n	e	s
i	j	k	m	l	b	i	s	h
r	e	m	i	q	k	r	p	i
p	c	a	r	e	f	u	l	o
o	t	a	l	l	e	s	t	e
r	n	s	w	u	h	e	j	a
t	m	o	r	n	i	n	g	w

© Harcourt

1. look
2. could
3. would
4. cook
5. book
6. boyhood
7. foot
8. childhood
9. stood
10. should
11. careful
12. chair
13. mountain
14. state
15. America

Handwriting Tip: Remember not to write letters too close together or too far apart.

Name _____

Words with *oo* and *ou*

▶ **Complete the sentences. Write a Spelling Word from the box on each line.**

cook	foot	book	childhood
stood	look	should	

1. Do you want to read my favorite

   _____?

2. We _____ on a bench to watch the parade.

3. Come and _____ at all the balloons!

4. You _____ always wear a helmet when you ride a bicycle.

5. Can you _____ oatmeal for breakfast?

6. I think you just stepped on my

   _____.

7. My grandmother had a happy

   _____ on a farm.

© Harcourt

Name _____

▶ Fill in the missing letters. Then write the Spelling Word.

1. st____ ____d   _____

2. c____ ____ld   _____

3. f____ ___t   _____

4. b____ ___k   _____

5. sh____ ____ld   _____

▶ Write the Spelling Words in ABC order.

state	look	chair	would	could

6. _____

7. _____

8. _____

9. _____

10. _____

SPELLING WORDS

1. look
2. could
3. would
4. cook
5. book
6. boyhood
7. foot
8. childhood
9. stood
10. should
11. careful
12. chair
13. mountain
14. state
15. America

SPELLING
STRATEGY
Try Different Spellings

Remember that some vowel sounds can be spelled more than one way.

1. look
2. could
3. would
4. cook
5. book
6. boyhood
7. foot
8. childhood
9. stood
10. should
11. careful
12. chair
13. mountain
14. state
15. America

Name _____

▶ **Word Shapes** Write a Spelling Word in each word shape. Then write the word.

1.

_____

2.

_____

3.

_____

4.

_____

▶ **Ask Me a Question** Answer each question with a Spelling Word.

5. What country do all Americans live in at some time?

_____

6. Where can people ski? _____

© Harcourt

Name _____

Words like *group* and *through*

▶ **Finish the story. Write a Spelling Word from the box on each line.**

through	youth	soup	group
throughway	routine	coupon	

1. A day of fun was planned for the

_____ of the town.

2. First, they saw a comedy _____ .

3. Then they rode a bus on the

_____ .

4. The children were given a _____ for the local toy store.

5. For lunch, the _____ stopped at a park.

6. They ate sandwiches and _____ .

7. Then everyone ran _____ the park.

SPELLING WORDS

1. routine
2. through
3. you
4. soup
5. group
6. wound
7. coupon
8. youth
9. throughway
10. throughout
11. childhood
12. should
13. able
14. board
15. seat

Handwriting Tip: When writing short letters, like *o* and *u*, make sure they sit on the bottom line and touch the midline.

soup

© Harcourt

1. routine
2. through
3. you
4. soup
5. group
6. wound
7. coupon
8. youth
9. throughway
10. throughout
11. childhood
12. should
13. able
14. board
15. seat

Proofread with a Partner

You can exchange papers with a partner and proofread each other's work.

Name _____

▶ **Draw a line through the misspelled word. Write the correct Spelling Word.**

1. board bord _____

2. woond wound _____

3. throogh through _____

4. shoold should _____

5. seat seet _____

▶ **Proofread this story draft. Circle the five misspelled words. Write the correct words. Not sure? Guess and check.**

Good Soup!

The yooth in our groep had soop for lunch. Yoo would think they hadn't eaten for days! Nobody talked at all throwout the entire lunch.

6. _____   7. _____

8. _____   9. _____

10. _____

© Harcourt

Name _____

▶ **Make Spelling Words by connecting the two word parts. Write the Spelling Words.**

through   tine   **1.** _____

cou   way   **2.** _____

child   out   **3.** _____

through   pon   **4.** _____

rou   hood   **5.** _____

▶ **Complete each sentence with a Spelling Word.**

6. Will you be _____ to help out on Saturday?

7. I have a _____ to buy jam.

8. Let's practice our _____ again.

9. We took the _____ to get to the mall.

10. _____ the summer, flowers grow in our yard.

© Harcourt

SPELLING WORDS
1. routine
2. through
3. you
4. soup
5. group
6. wound
7. coupon
8. youth
9. throughway
10. throughout
11. childhood
12. should
13. able
14. board
15. seat

SPELLING WORDS

1. crawled
2. saw
3. caught
4. seesaw
5. draw
6. lawn
7. naughty
8. taught
9. daughter
10. yawn
11. throughout
12. coupon
13. hole
14. night
15. story

Handwriting Tip: When you write the letter *w*, make sure it does not look like the letter *v*.

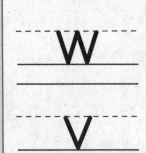

Words like *draw* and *caught*

▶ Write the Spelling Words in ABC order. If the first letters are the same, look at the second letters.

| saw crawled caught daughter |
| lawn naughty taught |

1. _____

2. _____

3. _____

4. _____

5. _____

6. _____

7. _____

▶ On each line, write the Spelling Word again.

8. yawn _____   9. draw _____

10. seesaw _____

© Harcourt

Name _____

▶ **Write a Spelling Word for each picture.**

1. _____

2. _____

3. _____

4. _____

▶ **Add three letters to make a Spelling Word. Then write the Spelling Word.**

5. There have been storms

thro____ ____ ____out the winter.

_____

6. The cat cau____ ____ ____ the

mouse. _____

7. How much is the co____ ____ ____n

worth? _____

SPELLING WORDS

1. crawled
2. saw
3. caught
4. seesaw
5. draw
6. lawn
7. naughty
8. taught
9. daughter
10. yawn
11. throughout
12. coupon
13. hole
14. night
15. story

SPELLING
STRATEGY
Picture a Word and Sound It Out

Think about the sound made by each letter and combination of letters.

© Harcourt

SPELLING WORDS

1. crawled
2. saw
3. caught
4. seesaw
5. draw
6. lawn
7. naughty
8. taught
9. daughter
10. yawn
11. throughout
12. coupon
13. hole
14. night
15. story

▶ Use the code to make Spelling Words.

1 = a	2 = r	3 = g	4 = s	5 = t
6 = e	7 = d	8 = h	9 = u	
10 = w	11 = y	12 = n		

1. 4-6-6-4-1-10 _____

2. 7-1-9-3-8-5-6-2 _____

3. 12-1-9-3-8-5-11 _____

4. 5-1-9-3-8-5 _____

▶ **Word Math** Write the Spelling Words.

5. laughter – l + d = _____

6. storm – m + y = _____

7. haughty – h + n = _____

8. cotton – tt + up = _____

▶ **Think About It** Which two Spelling Words are made up of two smaller words?

9. _____   **10.** _____

Name _____

Words That Begin with
over- and un-

▶ Complete each sentence. Write a Spelling Word from the box on each line.

> unfold overdue unsure overboard
> unfriendly overnight unfair overhead

1. I am _____ how to answer your question.

2. They threw the anchor _____.

3. The rules of the game are _____.

4. The growling dog is _____.

5. Alex mailed the package _____.

6. My homework is _____ by one day.

7. Look at the rain clouds forming

   _____.

8. Mom asked me to _____ my shirt and hang it up.

SPELLING WORDS

1. overdue
2. overnight
3. overboard
4. overflow
5. overhead
6. unfriendly
7. unsure
8. uneven
9. unfair
10. unfold
11. daughter
12. yawn
13. hungry
14. group
15. above

Handwriting Tip: When you write the letter *r*, make sure it does not look like an *n*.

© Harcourt

1. overdue
2. overnight
3. overboard
4. overflow
5. overhead
6. unfriendly
7. unsure
8. uneven
9. unfair
10. unfold
11. daughter
12. yawn
13. hungry
14. group
15. above

SPELLING
STRATEGY
Beginnings

To spell words
with prefixes,
think of the
spelling of the
base word, then
add the prefix at
the beginning.

Name _____

▶ **Add the prefix to each base word. Write the Spelling Word.**

1. (over) board   _____

2. (un) fair   _____

3. (un) even   _____

4. (over) night   _____

5. (un) friendly   _____

▶ **Circle the misspelled word in each sentence. Then write the Spelling Word correctly.**

6. If I yaun again, I am going to bed.

_____

7. Are you as hungrey as I am? _____

8. Store your books on the shelf abuv

mine. _____

9. Jenny is Mrs. Alvirez's daugter.

_____

10. You should join our groop. _____

© Harcourt

Name _____

▶ **Decode the Words** Look at the code. Then write the Spelling Word.

1. overdue
2. overnight
3. overboard
4. overflow
5. overhead
6. unfriendly
7. unsure
8. uneven
9. unfair
10. unfold
11. daughter
12. yawn
13. hungry
14. group
15. above

♡ = over	☆ = un

1. ♡ + due = _____

2. ☆ + even = _____

3. ☆ + sure = _____

4. ☆ + fair = _____

5. ♡ + flow = _____

▶ **A Puzzle** Write the correct Spelling Words in the puzzle. Use the clues.

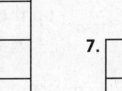
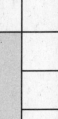

DOWN

6. undecided
7. not level
8. to flood

ACROSS

9. late
10. not right

© Harcourt

Name _____

Practice Test

▶ Read each sentence. Find the correctly spelled word that completes the sentence. Fill in the circle in front of that word.

Example: We had to _____ the map.
⬭ unfooled　　　⬭ unfolde　　　⚫ unfold

1. This _____ will save us money.
⬭ coupon　　　⬭ coopon　　　⬭ couppon

2. The project is _____.
⬭ overdue　　　⬭ overdoo　　　⬭ overdu

3. Drink water _____ the day.
⬭ threwout　　　⬭ thoughout　　　⬭ throughout

4. The spider _____ up the wall.
⬭ crawled　　　⬭ crauled　　　⬭ craughled

5. We can _____ this apple.
⬭ shair　　　⬭ share　　　⬭ shere

6. When _____ we come over?
⬭ should　　　⬭ shood　　　⬭ shoud

7. That was very _____ of you.
⬭ nawty　　　⬭ naugty　　　⬭ naughty

© Harcourt

Name_____

▶ **Read each sentence. Find the underlined Spelling Word that is spelled correctly. Fill in the circle below it.**

Example: The <u>airplane</u> flew <u>throuhg</u> the clouds.
                       ━━   ⬭

1. This <u>book</u> is <u>overdoo</u>.
        ⬭   ⬭

2. Were you <u>hapier</u> in your <u>childhood</u>?
           ⬭   ⬭

3. Many <u>airplains</u> fly in and out of this <u>city</u>.
         ⬭   ⬭

4. Mr. Tai's <u>daugter</u> now lives in <u>America</u>.
         ⬭   ⬭

5. Be <u>carfull</u> the bathtub does not <u>overflow</u>.
        ⬭   ⬭

6. The fox was <u>carful</u> not to get <u>caught</u> in the trap.
          ⬭   ⬭

7. You <u>should</u> <u>unfowld</u> your napkin.
        ⬭   ⬭

8. The legs on the <u>chare</u> are <u>uneven</u>.
           ⬭   ⬭

9. In the <u>morning</u>, the sun rises behind that <u>mowntain</u>.
        ⬭   ⬭

10. <u>Would</u> you like to ride on the <u>seasaw</u> with me?
      ⬭   ⬭

© Harcourt

Spelling Table

THE SPELLING TABLE below lists all the sounds that we use to speak the words of English. Each first column of the table gives the pronunciation symbol for a sound, such as **ō**. Each second column of the table gives an example of a common word in which this sound appears, such as *open* for the /ō/ sound. Each third column of the table provides examples of the ways that a sound can be spelled, such as *oh, o, oa, ow,* and *oe* for the /ō/ sound.

The Sound	As In	Is Spelled As
a	add	cat
ā	age	game, rain, day, paper
ä	palm	ah, father, dark, heart
â(r)	care	dare, fair, where, bear, their
b	bat	big, cabin, rabbit
ch	check	chop, march, catch
d	dog	dig, bad, ladder, called
e	egg	end, met, ready, any, said, says, friend
ē	equal	she, eat, see, key, city
f	fit	five, offer, cough, photo
g	go	gate, bigger
h	hot	hope, who
i	it	inch, hit
ī	ice	item, fine, pie, high, try, eye
j	joy	jump, gem, cage, edge

© Harcourt

The Sound	As In	Is Spelled As
k	keep	king, cat, lock
l	look	let, ball
m	move	make, hammer
n	nice	new, can, funny, know
ng	ring	thing, tongue
o	odd	pot, honor
ō	open	oh, over, go, oak, grow, toe
ô	dog	for, more, roar, ball, walk, dawn, fault
oi	oil	noise, toy
o͝o	took	foot, would
o͞o	pool	cool, soup, through, due, fruit, drew
ou	out	ounce, now
p	put	pin, cap, happy
r	run	red, car, hurry, wrist
s	see	sit, loss, listen, city
sh	rush	shoe, sure, ocean, special
t	top	tan, kept, better, walked
th	thin	think, cloth
t̶h̶	this	these, clothing
u	up	cut, butter, does, young
û(r)	burn	turn, bird, work, early, herd
v	very	vote, over, of
w	win	wait, towel
y	yet	year, onion
yo͞o	use	cue, few
z	zoo	zebra, lazy, buzz, was, scissors
zh	vision	garage, television
ə		about, listen, pencil, melon, circus

Spelling Strategies

Let us show you some of our favorite spelling strategies!

Here's a tip that helps me spell a word. First, I **say** the word. Next, I **picture** the way it is spelled. Then, I **write** it!

When I'm learning to spell a word, the **Study Steps to Learn a Word** on pages 8 and 9 are a big help.

I think of ways to spell the vowel sound in a word. Then I **try different spellings.**

When I don't know how to spell a word, sometimes I just take my best **guess!** Then I **check** it.

Sometimes I look up a word in the **dictionary.** Sometimes I just **ask someone** how to spell it.

© Harcourt

I **proofread** my work **twice.** First, I circle words I know are misspelled. Then I look for words I'm not sure of.

I look for **homophones** and make sure each word I've written **makes sense.**

Thinking of a **rhyming word** often helps me figure out how to spell a word. Both words may belong to the same word family.

Drawing the **shape** of a word helps me remember how to spell it. This is the shape of the word

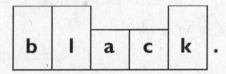

b l a c k .

When I'm writing a **compound word,** I think about how the **two smaller words** are spelled. That makes it easier!

When I need to spell **contractions,** I think about which **letters** have been **left out.** That's where I put the **apostrophe.**

I try to remember **rules,** such as making the right changes before adding <u>s</u> or <u>es</u>.

© Harcourt

My Spelling Log

WHAT'S A SPELLING LOG? It's a special place for words that are important to you. Look at what you will find in your Spelling Log!

Spelling Words to Study

This is the place for you to list words you need to study. There is a column for each unit of your spelling book.

My Own Word Collection

Be a word collector, and keep your collection here! Group words any way you like!

Sound Words

Cheerful Words

Social Studies Words

Vacation Words

Music Words

Funny Words

Animal Words

Math Words

© Harcourt

Spelling Words to Study

List the words from each lesson that need your special attention. Be sure to list the words that you misspelled on the Pretest.

Theme 1	Theme 2
Words with *id* and *ide*	Words with *ack* and *ock*
Words with *ame* and *ake*	Words like *earn* and *learn*
Words That End with *-ed*	Common Abbreviations
Words That End with *-ed* (*y* to *i*)	Words like *four* and *your*
Words with *at* and *ate*	Words with *ar*, *arm*, and *ark*

© Harcourt

Spelling Words to Study

Theme 3	Theme 4
Words with *ear* and *eer*	Words with *ou* and *ow*
Words with *spr*, *str*, and *thr*	Words with *oi* and *oy*
Words like *roots* and *food*	Words with *oo* and *ue*
Words with *gn*, *kn*, and *wr*	Plurals with *-es*
Words That End with *-s*, *-es*, and *-ies*	Words That End with *-ing* and *-ly*

© Harcourt

Spelling Words to Study

Theme 5	Theme 6
Words That Begin with *re-* and *pre-*	Words with *air* and *are*
Contractions	Words with *oo* and *ou*
Words with *ew* and *ui*	Words like *group* and *through*
Words with *gh* and *ph*	Words like *draw* and *caught*
Words That End with *-er* and *-est*	Words That Begin with *over-* and *un-*

My Own Word Collection

When you read and listen, find words you want to remember. Put the words into groups, and write them on these pages. Soon you will have a word collection of your very own!

My Own Word Collection

Save words you really like in My Own Word Collection. Include words that are hard for you to spell.

My Own Word Collection

Add a clue beside a word to help you remember it. The clue might be a picture, a sentence, a definition, or just a note.

© Harcourt

Handwriting
Manuscript Alphabet

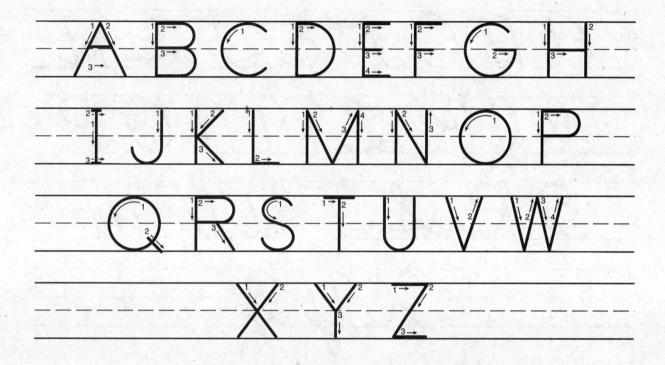

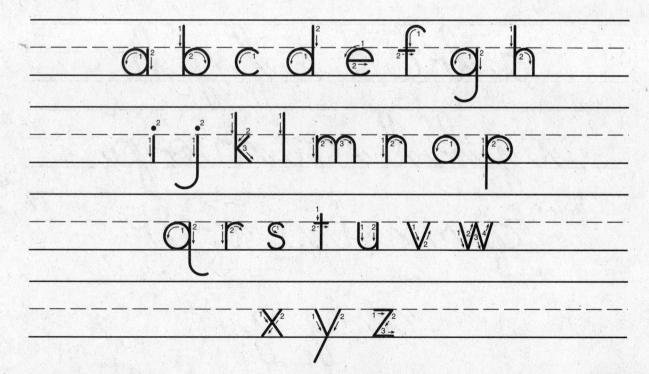

© Harcourt

Handwriting
Cursive Alphabet

A B C D E F G H
I J K L M N O P
2 R S T U V W
X Y Z

a b c d e f g h
i j k l m n o p
q r s t u v w
x y z

HANDWRITING MODELS

Handwriting
D'Nealian Manuscript Alphabet

A B C D E F G H
I J K L M N O P
Q R S T U V W
X Y Z

a b c d e f g h
i j k l m n o p
q r s t u v w
x y z

© Harcourt

Handwriting
D'Nealian Cursive Alphabet

A B C D E F G H

I J K L M N O P

Q R S T U V W

X Y Z

a b c d e f g h

i j k l m n o p

q r s t u v w

x y z